Let's face it,
being a baby isn't
all it's cracked
up to be.

From the moment you arrive

things
go straight
downhill.

You get poked
and prodded

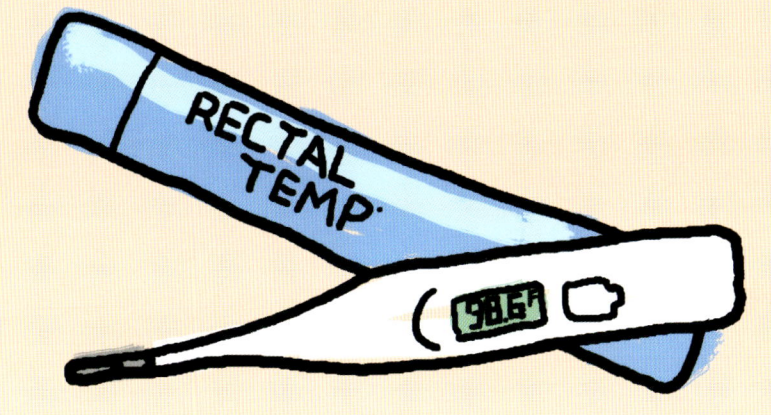

and inspected from every angle.

You're practically eaten alive!

Nothing makes
any sense.

Clothing
isn't optional

and most of the time it's downright uncomfortable.

You're either
too hot . . .

or too cold,

or some miserable
combination
of both.

It's all
some kind of
weird game

and without a
doubt the joke's
on you.

In the name
of safety . . .

you will
have no fun
whatsoever.

The coolest
toys will always
be just out of reach

and despite
your best
efforts,

LIFE IS POOP™

you'll still wind up empty handed.

LIFE IS POOP™

Grownups tend to overreact,

LIFE IS POOP™

and they love to say the word "No."

NO!
DON'T
DROP THAT RIGHT NOW
TAKE THAT OUT OF YOUR MOUTH
TIME TO TAKE YOUR MEDICINE!
REST TIME

LIFE IS POOP™

It can be
confusing,

LIFE IS POOP™

and, at times,
unpleasant.

LIFE IS POOP™

But it gets even worse.

LIFE IS POOP™

Unexpected stuff happens . . .

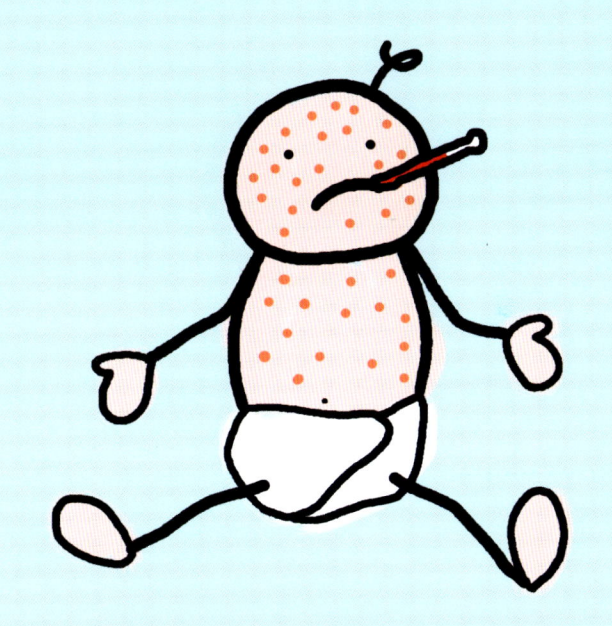

LIFE IS POOP™

and there's nothing you can do about it.

LIFE IS POOP™

So don't cry.

LIFE IS POOP™

Just dust
yourself off,

LIFE IS POOP™

accept what
comes your way,
and remember . . .

LIFE IS POOP™

Life is poop,
and we all
do our time.

LIFE IS POOP™